FAMILY MATTERS

FAMILY MATTERS

POEMS

ANNE MULVEY

BLUE BOAT BOOKS

2021

Family Matters
©2021 by Anne Mulvey

ISBN 978-1-7320804-3-0

First edition 2021
Printed in the United States of America

Cover art: *Simple Routines* (detail) by Sharon McCartney
Cover art photograph: John Polak
Cover design: Susan Kapuscinski Gaylord & Brendan Gaylord

Book interior design: Susan Kapuscinski Gaylord
Author photo: Susan Kapuscinski Gaylord
Text set in Eidetic Neo

Blue Boat Books
Jeri Kroll, Editor
Ipswich, Massachusetts 01938
email: krolljeri@gmail.com

Dedicated to
Rhina P. Espaillat
Mentor, muse, kindred spirit, and dear friend

In memory of
Pat Schneider
Alive in our hearts and in our stories
(1934-2020)

CONTENTS

Reckoning

I was the second child,
second girl, second of six
or third of eight,
depending
on how one counted.

I was taught I was less
and to want to be least.
I wanted to be more
and to know that I was.
I was counting, and wanting to.

CHANGE

The egg man came to our front door,
brought us two dozen every Saturday,
made change from the bank that hung from his belt
clanging quarters, nickels, pennies, and dimes.

The cleaning lady used the back door,
went down to the basement where she
pulled her clothes from a plain brown bag
and made her change without a sound.

Was it the dirty work she did for us
or the color she couldn't change?

HARTFORD, CT, JULY 6, 1944

Elephants. Smoke. Flames. Bertha
grabs four-year-old Miriam's arm, yanks
her from the aisle, grips Marjorie's
wrist—*I'll reach as far as I can*
drop you   catch your sister   the baby.
Wait there   don't move! Bertha slips
her nine-year-old in between
the bleacher slats, stretches, lets go,
dangles and drops Miriam, David.
She squeezes through last, lets go.

Marjorie, Miriam, David, Bertha
crawling   face down   inhaling smoke
tasting dirt, an eight-legged human
lifeline inching away from clogged
exits to the tent's edge, slipping
under canvas between pilings and stakes.
Away from flames toward summer sun,
Bertha hurries her children home.

One hundred sixty-eight people died.
Miriam still feels the imprint
of her mother's hand on her arm.

BURNING BRIGHT

Eyes retreat to back of bony sockets.
Deep pockets hold black moons.
Ebony globes burn bright.
Strobe lights haunt the day,
search the night. Death mask,
the doctor calls it. Soon
you are gone except for the hole
burning in my heart.

SLOW

I was always a slow eater.
Ask anyone who has known me.
I rarely bite off more than I can chew,
and chew each morsel through and through.

I'm slow to heal from stress
fractures, aches, all kinds of pain.
It should come as no surprise
that grieving goes on and on,
and mourning is so slow
that no one wants to know.

It takes a long time to swallow
such a hard meal, much longer to heal.

Irish-American

Shamrocks and leprechauns, wee fairies in the wood.
Irish need not apply, know your place and be good.
Religion and song—the English were wrong.
Shanty or lace curtain, we were never certain,
being Irish.

The German grocer said that he could see
the map of Ireland on me.
I saw rivers and roads, mountains,
green fields, shamrocks growing wild.
Were his eyes or my mirror telling lies?

I asked my mother. She told me
I share a look with others near and far.
She told me that the Irish come
not just with freckles, red hair, eyes blue.

Mother said there are Black Irish—
black hair, black as the ace of spades,
the darkest of eyes, and skin
that doesn't turn red in the sun.
She told me from where we had come.

Mother told of Spanish ships flung up
against rough rocky cliffs. The Armada,
she called it. Wrecked vessels spilled
treasures on an Irish strand, mixing Celts
with tribes from another land.

Legacies of war and of riches,
of loss and of survival on new shores.
Being Irish took on a darker hue
and linked me to the sea so black, so blue.

Mother knew the grocer's map
was not a map at all. And now I do—
so when someone says they see a map
of Ireland on me, I see it too.

Shamrocks and leprechauns, wee fairies in the wood.
Irish need not apply, know your place and be good.
Religion and song—the English were wrong.
Shanty or lace curtain, we were never certain,
being American.

WILLFUL

The nurses told Mother it was
a blessing in disguise, a godsend,
though God had not sent, but taken.
They called it Monster, not him or her.
The doctor told Mother she wouldn't,
she couldn't, have more. She already
had one, better than none. None would be
better than that one, the one who was
to be and not to be. The nurses said,
Spontaneous abortion is God's will.
Sent and taken. Not meant to be. Monster.

A year later against great odds, despite
God's will, spontaneous and meant to be,
the monster's sister came. She is me.

RECYCLING CIRCA 1950

When we outgrew wading pools
and sprinklers wouldn't do, we'd swim
in deeper seas thanks to World War II.

Guppies turned tadpoles, slippery Seabees
landlocked in the backyard, we paddled hard
fore and aft in our Navy surplus raft.

Avoiding land mines, we'd swim for miles
submarine style and surface all smiles,
our only battle scars blue-green stripes
rubbed off sea's sides and worn with pride—
granted our wish to be fancier fish.

WALKING DOWNTOWN

Waterfall swallows words, wraps ears,
juggles day and night, night and day.
Wind slings liquid knives, splits hairs,
baffles all the way. Stilt-walking
trestle hands out slivers, dances solo,
kicks up heels with any partner,
rhumbas only with train. Defying death,
we walk the tight-rope over waves,
swing trapeze with ease, make magic.
I am safe. Daddy holds my hand.

HOLDING COURT, BROOKLYN, 1953

Aunt Fiona and I are at the back
of a room with dark brown benches.
Uncle Ted is sitting up front
at a desk wearing a black robe.
I'm almost seven, old enough
to see my godfather be a judge.

He's talking to a colored man.
The man's head is down, his shoulders
are too. I don't know what's going on.
It started before we got here.
I think the colored man stole food
from a stand or cart outside.
I think he grabbed something and ran away
so no one would catch him, but someone did.

Uncle Ted sees us, smiles, and waves.
I smile. He whispers to a man
wearing a black uniform and a badge.
We follow that man to the front
of the long room right past the colored man.
My uncle gives us front row seats.

The judge tells the colored man,
*Never take anything again
without paying or you'll be sorry.
I'll let you off easy this time.
Did you think you could steal and get away
with it? Don't you know right from wrong?*

The bench that I wanted to see
is just a chair way up high.
I don't like being here watching
my godfather be the judge.
My uncle says he'll meet us at Schrafft's,
buy me ice cream, any kind I want.
I love ice cream and my Uncle Ted,
but I can't decide what I want.

LEONA'S PLACE

The place where Leona lived
wasn't far from where we lived,
but no one ever went there—
how far it seemed, how close it was.

On scorching summer days, the narrow road
was thick with dirt—dust stuck to teeth.
The houses looked like summer
cottages that had seen better days,
but they weren't near the river or lakes.

Rockers and sagging chairs sat on
stamp-sized porches. Daisies sagged and fell
from air too hot to breathe. Sunflowers
shadowed homes they grew against.
Old people rocked. Kids played. Dogs roamed.

On Tuesdays when Leona came to clean,
she took the bus. In bad weather,
Mom drove Leona back to her place.
I always wanted to go—I was
looking for a home myself
and a way to get out, too.

EGGING: A SPLIT SECOND

A split second after playing
with my best friend (an only child
whose mother wanted to play with us),
the breeze said, *Go back, get your sweater.*
I knocked, opened the door a crack,
just enough to see them sitting close,
and to hear her mother say,
She was egging to stay. Egging?

Humpty Dumpty appeared perched
precariously on a wall. An egg
cracked over my head (maybe inside?).
Silent, its shell shattered in smithereens
spilling shards too tiny to see.

I didn't think the steps would be sticky.
I felt the broken yolk that stuck
to my shoes and dribbled down
egging the green grass yellow. My shoes
unstuck enough that I escaped.

Afraid I'd break my mother's back,
I ran home fast skipping over
every crack. Never went back.

PRESENT

Replaying the past,
projecting the future,
all that's lost is the present
and my presence.

Letting go of the past,
not worrying about the future,
all that's left is the present
and my presence. All that.

How Good It Was

Mother told us how good it was
that Wilma went to the new IU
extension campus. It wasn't
a campus, just a building, no frills
or football like Notre Dame,
but it did have a river view.

Mother told us how good it was
Wilma wanted to be a teacher.
Now Mom wonders if Wilma did
become a teacher. Back then Wilma
came to our house every day
except weekends when Dad was home.
I wanted Wilma to be like family,
but she was just "a mother's helper."
I was, too, but without the "a"
that got in the way of being family.

Wilma came before Terry when Mom
was big, number six on the way,
number six who came at the end
of a hot summer, the end
of the fifties. Wilma took two buses
to get from her side to ours.
It took Wilma hours carrying
big books, pencils, and pens wearing
a stiff, starched, bright-white uniform
looking like a nurse, prim and proper.

I wanted Wilma to wear shorts
and sleeveless tops that wouldn't wilt with heat.
I loved to look at Wilma's face shining
dark beauty against starched white,
her arms strong and firm, and her hands
when they stopped next to mine at lunch.
We shared sandwiches and milk,
few words, smiles, unasked questions—
Do you like volleyball, swimming?
When's your birthday? What's your favorite food,
game, color? Do you like to sing?

Wilma came when I was ten,
a little girl hungry for smiles
and full of questions. She left
when I was twelve. I wished Wilma
would stay and play. How good it was,
but not as good as it could have been.

I WAS A LITTLE GIRL

The Cave Kids (all boys) crossed the tracks,
each brandishing a slingshot. I was
a little girl and meant to be afraid.
Jimmy Carpenter, who lived next door,
raised his BB gun when I walked by.
I was a little girl and meant to be
afraid. My brothers shot their cap guns—
I jumped. They laughed. When I was a little
girl, I was afraid. Now, I'm not.

Denim Plus

I loved denim from my first pair of jeans
when denim was only dark blue before
anyone imagined paying big bucks
for pre-shredded designer jeans
and before stores sold ten styles—
straight leg, bell bottom, comfort fit,
and more—before there was a classic
since classic was all there was
and denim was only for jeans
and Western shirts held tight by tiny
round white pearlescent snaps.

My favorite denim was the bottom
of my two-piece bathing suit—
short shorts that covered just enough
to not see crotch or ride up butt,
but left waist and midriff bare
to barely below my budding breasts
where madras plaid began and went
almost to my clavicle—
denim plus madras, a fifties fad,
comfort and fashion that looked good on me.

The doctor said the tumor was
too big for a bikini cut.
I didn't want one anyway.

High Hopes Circa 1960

We heard the bells that told us to wake up,
get dressed, eat breakfast. We followed bells
that told us where to go and when to kneel,
to pray, and even what to say. They chimed
in chapel time, Holy Mass, then school,
study hall, choir rehearsal, chores,
play till it was time to pray again,
dinner, dishes, silence, lights out, then sleep
till bells at dawn awake. Chime by chime,
those mundane bells kept track of earthly time.

Wedding bells had lured teen girls from home
to offer hearts and souls for perfect love.
Celestial bells had swept us off our feet.
Soon we'd be brides of Christ, and marry up.

For Patricia, Whose Hair
I Straightened in 1962

When you arrived, I wondered if you'd like
Ancilla Domini Convent School
where, like us, you'd wear blue serge
uniforms, so dark as to be black,
with white blouses. You'd live by bells,
have meals all together after grace,
do everything together.
Every six weeks, you'd be assigned
a new roommate. You'd have to keep your door
open all the time, both day and night.

Some doors cannot be easily opened.
Some currents cannot be stilled.
Even hair can be charged.
Your mother made the nuns promise
yours would be straightened every week.
I was chosen to care for your hair.

Saturdays at nine, I washed your hair,
rubbed pomade onto your waves,
and reached in with a hot comb,
afraid I wouldn't get to the roots
or—worse—would singe the nape
of your neck, or scorch your scalp.
I know I burned you sometimes.
You'd cringe, but say, *It didn't hurt.*
You never complained.

I wanted to know your family,
your dreams. I didn't want to pry.
I wanted to do your hair
the way your mother would have liked.
One day, you were gone. Left.
I still wonder why.

FOR DENISE, WHO WAS UPWARD BOUND FROM LAKE FOREST TO CHICAGO

Denise, I've wondered how you are
since that sultry summer of '66.
You missed your momma and Bobby too,
grieved for the South Side and those you knew.
Did you go back to Hyde Park High?

I finished college in '68,
went west to San Francisco
singing "California Dreamin'"–
couldn't find a job when I got there.

Did you graduate in '68–
was your period simply late?
I meant to stay in touch after
that sultry summer of '66.

I wonder how you are, Denise.
I hope it's not too late to tell you so.

If Only

If you weren't afraid of death,
would it change your life?
Probably.

But how would you know that you weren't
afraid, or that your life had changed?

If you weren't afraid of life,
would it change your death?
Probably.

But how would you know that you weren't
afraid, or that your death had changed?

LOVE IN THE MAKING

I do not remember how long
it had been since I saw you undress.
I know that it had been a long, long time.

I remember
the baby body
the changing table
the smell
the mess—
chafing cream soothing
your skin so soft.

I remember
the boy body
skinny as nails
gawky
growing
exploding
grown-up beauty.

I remember
the man body
full shoulders
hips tight
virile
graceful
male beauty.

I remember the nurse asking
did you want us to leave and your grin
speaking with you, *Nah, I'm not modest.*

I remember laughing then
together in our closeness
as sisters and brothers are.

I remember the doctor asking you
about sex, intercourse.
I don't remember the word she used.
I was embarrassed. You weren't.

No problem. Shooting blanks, though.
I remember the rakish twinkle
in your eye. Then you mentioned the pain.
I remember your dying body
collapsing on the table—
the smell, the mess. No cream
could soothe your parchment skin.

I remember your beautiful being.
I remember the pain.
I remember love in the making.
Michael, I remember.

BEN SHERMAN HILL, ROUTE 64

March 17, 1994

We got the call after we'd left
you with green balloons from Mom and Dad,
a leprechaun from me, and a giant
green nose from your best buddy Spencer
who'd flown in in the nick of time.

We got the call in the middle
of dinner pretending that it was
St. Patrick's Day like it used to be—
corned beef and cabbage, shamrock cookies,
Smithwick's, Jameson's, Bailey's,
and Carmel Quinn singing "Galway Bay."

We dashed to the car when we got the call.
We rushed up this hill that night,
Ben Sherman Hill, Route 64, hoping
there'd be more time. Spencer was driving
way too fast, or way too slow.
I wanted to yell, *Spencer, slow down,
you'll hit the bank, miss a curve.*
I wanted to scream, *Spence, speed up,
there might not be much time!* I was sitting
behind Dad next to Mom holding
her hand, squeezing it for dear life.
I didn't want to scare them.

We made it in time, but barely.
You called to the kids, *Good night.*
I drove them down Ben Sherman Hill,
Route 64. It was snowing.
I was terrified we'd slide off the road
or you'd be gone before I got them home.
I got them home. I hope that you did, too.

November 23, 1997

I'm still holding Mother's hand.
Dad inches closer to you each day.
This morning, I left to go back home.
I left in the dark. I wanted
the sun to warm the morning.
I wanted to watch the sun rise
just past this hill, Ben Sherman Hill,
Route 64. I wanted more, wanted
to see more, wanted to speed up
in the light, but it was slippery
and gray. I'm sipping hot coffee
from the Lady Bug mug you loved.
The sun didn't come up the way
I wanted it to, but it did come up.

VICIOUS AUNTIE

Way back when Grammy June was just a girl,
her nephew called her Vicious Auntie.
Billy was six months younger.
They played together all the time.

Vicious Auntie? Well, yes—she was
quite the tomboy way back then.
You wouldn't know it now for all her fears.
She was the youngest of seven.
Carrie, the oldest, was married
by the time Vicious Auntie arrived.

I was the only one of us
born in a hospital. After all,
by then, Mumma was at least
forty-seven, maybe forty-eight.
Yes, that was in old Marblehead
before they had to sell the farm.
That was before Papa died.
Papa was a good businessman.
Everybody liked him. Saturday
mornings, he'd take me with him
to Swampscott to deliver chickens.

I loved seeing the fancy houses
in Clifton. Some of the people
invited me in, gave me something
good to eat, something sweet.
They were always nice to me.
Yes, that was a long time ago
before Papa died, and Mumma, too.

That was way back when we had the farm
overlooking Hooper's Field in old
Marblehead. We still had the farm
high up on the hill full of fruit trees—
apple, cherry, and pear. We climbed
white birches that carried us back
to the ground. Vicious Auntie goes on.

Cancers

It's a cancer on the body politic.
Kill it, kill it now before it spreads.
House Manager, *Impeachment Hearings,* 1998

We are watching cancer spread
through June, through her body
that's turning against itself, turning
against her, binding us together.

We're sick of watching white males,
each one holier than the last until
the next report reports more threats,
more leaks, more sleaze. Stop it—please!

We stop reading the newspapers.
We turn off the television.
We don't watch the body politic.

That body may be hurtful, harmful,
heartless, merciless to the hungry,
the homeless, the hopeless.

But it is not cancer.
Do not use that word. Don't
take that name, that pain, in vain.

We move nightgowns, towels, sheets
—heavy, wet, cold, and clean—
from the washer to the dryer.

We simmer chicken, stripping it
to the bone to flavor broth.
We offer sips of sustenance
hoping for a change, for June.

MORE

To like, to love—
Is it that easy?
Is it that hard?

To like, to love—
Is it that simple?
Is it that complex?

To like, to love—
Is that all there is to it?
Is there all that to it?

Ah, yes—both, all, and always more.

REBELS

Rebel, named for the Easter Rebellion,
you came when we were so alone.
You picked a clan that suited you, the one
that needed you to make their house a home.

From Mishawaka to Woodbury—
open spaces, huge skies, Indiana's
heartlands shrink miles behind the car.
Closed in in Connecticut—that's us.

Our parents promised us a special dog
when they told us that we had to come.
The pick of the litter; you'll want to stay.
No way, we cried, pouting and glum.

They talk funny and have lots of money.
We wanna go back home where we belong.
We want a choice! Give us a voice!
Pushed, then prodded, we moved along.

We'd had some troubles, don't get me wrong—
but soon we'd sing a happy song.

When you arrived, Rebel, you led the way
to treasures far beyond our door.
Whenever you came home, we'd return
by your side, satisfied once more.

We'd watch you leap across the fields
your auburn coat blazing bright light—
retrieving sticks, balls, bones, then back
in a flash of sheer delight.

Diving into the Pomperaug to swim,
then shaking and shimmering with spray,
you'd bring back the stones we skipped
and sometimes prey, expanding play.

We'd had troubles, things seemed all wrong—
but now we sing a happy song.

You leaped before Daddy could say, *Stay,*
the day the leash wound round his leg.
And then when he was near, we'd hear
the cast go "thump" like a wooden peg.

As years went by, your stature grew.
Your feet began to slow. Your coat grew thin.
The town now had our hearts, and so did you.
Your time was through. There was no more to win.

We fed you favorite foods, stayed near,
then said goodbye, and held you till the end.
We cried. We laughed. We tell your story still.
Our lives went on with duties to attend.

We'd had some troubles, but we moved on—
and we continued with our song.

* * *

Michael, named after Grandpa who'd just died,
you came and soon became our rebel.
As frisky as a puppy but a boy,
babysitting for you was terrible.

At four you hid inside the car
lighting matches out of sight. You blew
out the flames, but left tell-tale embers
smoldering so Mom and Dad soon knew.

At five when you broke into Nana's house
looking for a treasure to hide,
footprints left a trail to Little Thief.
But Nana's ring is still buried outside.

When Peggy came to live with us,
at Sunday dinners after Mass,
you'd slip silver spoons into her pocket.
Why did you steal my spoon, you'd ask.

You'd pour cold coke into hot coffee.
Soon bubbles would gurgle up
and down onto the lace tablecloth,
and doubling bubbling giggles would erupt.

We'd had some troubles, don't get me wrong—
this isn't only a happy song.

In time you'd perfected your wayward ways
playing hooky, smoking, speeding, barfing,
farting, surprises, disguises.
In everything, you were leading.

You had such fun with everyone.
We'd laugh so hard that soon we'd cry.
At home, outside, both friend and foe
like bees to honey, all would fly.

Rebel the man, you knew what mattered most.
Your heart sure knew you wanted Sue.
Mother came 'round, but oh, so slow.
You grew a family. We loved them too.

Deadhead who danced so gratefully,
you coached your kids, taught shop at school.
You lived so high and didn't die.
You played the fool but, oh, so cool.

We'd had some troubles, oh, yes, that's right—
and soon we'd face that long dark night.

When Susie's sister Sally died,
we looked across the chapel space
and wondered why you had that stare
and graying hair, and Grandpa's face.

Rebel, daredevil, we thought you'd smash
a wall, alcohol, a brawl—but sick?
We thought you were invincible.
You went so slow. You went so quick.

Michael, dear rebel, you fought so hard,
gave all you could with grit and grace.
You gave us all so much, but left so much
empty. You gave so much, but left our place.

We'd had some troubles, oh, yes, that's right—
and then we faced that long dark night.

AT 80

At 80 she is learning
to cook again
for her husband
of 53 years

vegetables and fruit
no salt
no spirits

I watch her stir
soul food
salted with
strong spirits

at 49 I am meeting
a mother
I did not know I had

MAIDEN AUNT

Your handkerchiefs are in the top drawer
of your dresser. The one on top has a
curlicue "E" in one corner. Blue
on a field of white, it holds its own
as you did living alone in Brooklyn.

"McM," hand-stitched on green linen
edged in white lace, highlights Irish roots,
reminding me of your gift of gab
and love of family. "Eleanor"
is embroidered on the next one.

Poinsettias point to Christmas,
happy holidays, pre-dawn wake-up calls,
shivering in the dark watching our breath
as we watched for the train from New York.
You crossed the Hudson and traveled
seven hundred miles to be with us!

A few handkerchiefs turn up covered
with dollies, airplanes, lollipops,
or antique trains. They looked as if
they belonged to a child. You had
so much fun playing with everyone.

Bigger and brighter than the others,
amber, brown, and burnt orange squares
pop up. Modern fashion statements, they are
bold, elegant, and sure of themselves.
You were small, but bright all right.

This well-worn one must have been
in service for a long time. Maybe
it was one you had when we watched
World War II movies on your TV.
I'd go through a box of tissues sobbing
between bites of chocolate from your freezer.

Underneath the others, threadbare and frayed,
are the plain white Irish linen hankies
you tucked under your sleeve most days.
Did Grandma or Aunt Jule give some
of them to you? They remind me
of our family as we used to be.

Now your handkerchiefs are gone, passed on
to someone else who's dear. Your grand-niece
will make something new with them, from you.
We'll remember the gifts you've shared
and the good times that we had—glad
that we had you, Aunt Eleanor McMahon.

On Turning 50

A new broom.
A pinch of salt.
A loaf of bread.

These are the things
my mother told me
to take to a new home.

A new broom sweeps clean.
Salt seasons.
Bread is life.

I used to take more.
I traveled burdened
by many things.

Turning on 50.
Back to basics.
Broom. Salt. Bread.

Swept clean.
Seasoned.
Life to share.

MULTILINGUAL

I heard a Cambodian poet read
a poem in Khmer that sounded like
chanting, like singing tears. In English
I asked her about the story I'd felt.
Her words stumbled back in my tongue.

After they came, everything changed.
I was just a child, barely a teen
watching all of it—everything.
She tells of guards, soldiers, deaths.
The poet says, *Sometimes, reading is hard*
because—as she points to her heart,
my hand jumps to mine. Then she tells me
her father and brothers were gone
before the story she sang began.

They made me marry, said I had to
marry a man I did not know.
The soldiers stood with guns pointed
at our backs. We had no choice.
I back away, breath gone, hand tight over
my breast. *There was nothing left.*
I ran and ran and ran toward Thailand
seven months pregnant. I was running
for my life, ours, my baby.

Her hands move down, make a half-moon
'round her belly. *I stumbled near*
the border. I stumbled, fell down hard
and the baby came too soon.
I was only nineteen and only
seven months pregnant. I did not know
if my mother and sisters were alive—
and my baby came too soon.
The shine from her tears reflected mine.

She reached into her purse for a picture.
She is standing next to a tall young man.
The young man is smiling, their arms entwined.
He's nineteen, she says. Tears flow
for the mother who'd sung her story
and for her "too soon" baby
born at the border who stands so tall.

Two Cambodian Poets Speak

She chants Khmer sounding, keening, wailing,
calling back to ancestors' bones still there,
still there in their homeland. She knows
the old ways, misses monsoon season,
how it was before and all it took
to make it here. She tells of flight,
of silencing her baby in the night
for fear the soldiers might. She misses
her sisters, and her mother's smile.
She wishes that her children knew many
they cannot, and wants them not
to know much of what they do.

He speaks only English, knows his culture
second hand, and mainly the worst of it.
His poems are bold, cold, hard spray-paint
pictures of things that we don't want to see.
He tells it like it is—as he's seen it,
felt it, known it deep in his orphan bones
in the good old US of A.
He knows too much about this land
of the brave where homes are never free,
rarely affordable. Wishing
he had a grandmother, he searches
the eyes of the old women
looking for the ones he lost.

She is not his mother, only by blood—
spilled blood, home blood, blood in irrigation
ditches, blood by borders that ran to camps
or sailed in flimsy boats abandoned
at the bottom of the ocean
or in a city of milk and honey
for the chosen, the chosen few.
The young man calls her his teacher,
the one who taught him his culture,
who told her stories, and told him
to tell his stories in his own words.

The Cambodian poets fold
borders to form blankets. Each
one translates for the other.

SAFETY IS . . .

Safety is another word for . . .

> peace, but not at any cost;
> quiet, but not the scary kind;
> enough of what you need,
> but not too much of what you don't—
> and love, the good kind.

Safety is peace, quiet, enough but not too much, and love.

THE SWIM BAG

Handed up from son to father,
the swim bag hangs in the garage.
Cruel legacy.
The bag was deep charcoal gray,
bright red trim. The pockets expanded
to hold everything needed then.

Now the gray's turned dirty white,
red faded pink, pockets stiff.
Compartments just confuse. Strap hangs loose
on the father's stooped shoulder.
More than frayed and almost empty,
the swim bag holds a pair of threadbare trunks,
a bar of soap, old goggles
(locker lock lost, pool pass misplaced).

They used to go together.
Each held his own, but then the son
took his final lap. Now the father
is taking his. The swim bag
is too small to hold it all.

TOE PARTIES

On Saturdays after pancakes and chores,
we had Toe Parties for three—
Daddy, Luke and me.

We had special seats. Mine was the edge
of the tub, Luke's the top of the step stool,
Daddy's the toilet seat, top down.

Luke's feet were little and mine were big.
Daddy's were so big they reached all the way
to ours—and his toes were giant.

The party started with a dance of feet
and toes slipping, sliding, gliding
across the bathroom ballroom floor stretching,
colliding, retreating, meeting.

When we were real little we played
"This Little Piggy." Puppet shows
came later with toes playing the roles
(Grumps, Bitsie, Taffy, Sassy, Silly).

Rounding up dirt, stealing sock lint
and shoveling sand from between our toes,
Daddy found buried treasures—diamonds,
emeralds, rubies, and gold doubloons.

Daddy would hammer away at our nails,
paint them with polka dots, rainbows and snails.
The grand finale was fancy footwork,
tapping toes, and knocking knees.

Back then a week seemed so long to wait,
but we knew that Daddy would check the chores
and then proclaim: *Toe Party for three—*
Kiera, Luke, and me!

My feet have doubled in size and Luke's
have outgrown mine. Our toes are bigger, too,
but they don't fill the room like Daddy's did.

He Remembers, and Doesn't

He remembers that he likes sports:
Notre Dame football the favorite,
and the Dodgers are his baseball team
though they moved to LA years ago.
He left Brooklyn before they did.

He remembers he likes to read,
stares at the *New York Times* for hours,
reads the same thing over and over
to anyone who will listen.

He remembers he likes ice cream
(vanilla with chocolate sauce) and cookies
(Fig Newtons and chocolate chip), but hates
whipped cream, so don't give him any.

He remembers he was the captain
of the Manhattan College Swim Team
Class of '37, and that he crawled
two hours each way by subway
through three boroughs just to get there.

He doesn't remember what to wear
though he dresses himself by himself
and brushes his teeth at least
twice a day, sometimes three or four.

He doesn't remember which cabinet
holds the cereal, but knows he wants
Special K every day with half
a banana sliced *Thin to win*
and a little milk that's skim.

He remembers his wife of fifty years,
still calling her, *My first wife.*
He's lost track of his children's names,
but always knows hers—Muriel.

He doesn't remember what jobs he had
or where he lived except Brooklyn
where he grew up, and Indiana
where he grew his family, roses,
apple blossoms, a cherry tree.

He doesn't remember what day it is.
He doesn't remember what he reads.
He doesn't remember which team just won.
He doesn't remember how to swim.

We got used to all that, but not
to his forgetting Michael.
When Daddy didn't remember
his child who'd died, that was the worst
again. But at least Dad didn't
remember he didn't remember.

In the End

There was little we could do in the end.
Flowers, balloons, TV on or off—
raise or lower the volume, the lights.
When the machines were finally quiet,
tubes out, mask and restraints removed,
we plunged a jagged pink sponge
on a lollipop stick to the bottom
of a cardboard cup. We swabbed your lips,
squeezed drops of water one by one
onto your tongue. We searched your eyes
and your face looking for final
directions, fatherly advice.
We wanted to know how much to give
in the end. If you could have,
you would have told us. We held your hand
the way that you used to hold ours.

CHRISTMAS EVE

I'm wearing your kid gloves, steel gray,
the ones that were on your dresser
the next day. They're much too big.
I squeeze my fingers as hard as I can
into the palms wanting to hold on.
I feel a chill slip through the hole
in my fleece pants, the ones that tore
sliding out of the ambulance.
The sign said to use the side door.
I wanted to stay with you,
but got stuck behind the stretcher.

Eleven days later on Christmas Eve,
fresh snow hangs every branch heavy.
The chilled air reveals my breath
reminding me of watching you
breathe out, breathe in, breathe out.

I knew that it was time for you to go.
I'm never ready for long trips.

Doing Dishes

She tells him to tap the top of each glass,
then give each one a single swipe
with a linen towel as soon
as the wash cycle stops before
the drying has begun. He tells her
to turn on the water first,
then let it run until it's piping hot
before turning on the dishwasher.

Both improve the flow of daily chores.
It's an art to know how to start
and when to stop.
Each in its way saves time or work,
a dollar or two, which makes good sense.

They are trading family secrets,
swapping recipes as they talk each night
over dishes and five hundred miles,
a mother and her son.

Her dishes are all done. He stands
at the sink doing dishes her way.
No phone connects him to her now,
but they are talking heart to heart.

TALKING BACK

At first, there was just one of you.
I couldn't have imagined two.
But then you said you had a son.
He was the only holy one.

Before I'd reached the age of reason,
you'd convinced me that it was treason
to doubt the holy trinity—
then I had three gods I could not see.

I wish I hadn't been so slow.
I wish I had decided long ago
to listen to just one instead of three,
hearing less from you and more from me.

GOLLY RAGS

Aspiring to be brides of Christ,
at 15 hardly teens ourselves,
we were given the sacred duty
of disposing of dirty secrets.
We called them "Golly Rags."
(We made up that name or maybe
our grown sisters, wives of Christ,
handed it down with the other duty
that we carried out once a week.)

We weren't to speak or to peek
while we took up the monthly
collection of crusted blood that reeked
and deposited the change not worth
saving, not sacred like the blood of Christ.
Sloughed off, discharged down the laundry chute,
Golly Rags were full of holes,
but they were not holy.

Only rags remained bleached clean,
absorbent and soft—nothing like
the round cotton collars starched stiff as boards
separating head from body and blood,
heart and soul. Natural rhythms breathe
beneath unnatural separations.
Transformed to Golly Rags, old collars came
full circle.
                    Transforming ourselves,
old crones haggle over interest due,
tell our own stories, rename rags.
Holding vessels of fruit from sacred wombs
and wounds, Golly Rags held body and blood,
heart and soul. Wholly holy.

SO WHAT . . .

So what if women are afraid
to go out alone at night?
So what if everybody knows, but
no body cares. So what if women
are afraid of being harassed and hurt
when men are afraid of not having
the woman they want when they want,
the way they want her, it, them.
So what if women are afraid
of being raped, murdered, when men
are afraid of being teased, rebuffed,
not tough enough, and it's all her fault, too,
for what she did or didn't do. So what?

So why is it that we divide
the world in two and then say who
has a right to the starry night.
So why is it women's anger
is not allowed, and why is men's
a holy shroud covering up
all kinds of findings, bodies
of knowledge lying there.

So what if women are afraid
of strangers behind bushes when it's
men they know, trust, live with,
marry, marry and leave—safe ones,
protectors, more likely to be
violators—protectors who
do it in the name of love,
do it in the name of war,
do it in the name of peace,

do it in the name of the father,
the son, all the holy men.

So what if women are afraid
but we blame nature, Adam's rib,
evil Eve, even when we know it's
here and now, abuse here now—
abuse of power, of privilege.
Not God's will, God's war, God's love—
not from above—and no kind of love.

So what else is so, so old?
So what else is so, so new?
So what in the world and in the home
is going on everywhere?
So what in the world is going on—
and why in the world is it?

LESSONS

My father taught me many things—
to ride a bike, rake leaves, skate, swim,
mow grass, recycle, and shine shoes.
Look at the stars, but watch where you're going.
Skip stones across the lake, but don't make waves.
Remember Dad's favorite quotes—
Consistency is the hallmark
of champions. Consistency
is the hobgoblin of small minds.
Say the rosary and pray every day
the one holy and apostolic way.
Memorize the periodic table.
Remember who you are (a child of God
or just a girl?) and where you're from
(God, Indiana, Ireland?).

I tried to be good and follow the rules—
When not in use turn off the juice, make ice,
be nice, take turns, and always do it right.
I tried to learn as hard as
my father tried to teach.

TRUTHS

My father called himself an orphan.
He said he'd never known his father.

My mother always disagreed:
Bill, you must have known your father.
When he died you weren't four or five—
you were at least seven or eight.
And you weren't an orphan.
You have a mother. He did, Nana,
who lived in a little cottage
behind our house, almost with us.

I knew that my mother was right,
but I felt my father's fatherlessness.
I wanted to bring his father back
from the Catskills where he died of TB.
When my father told this story,
his eyes glistened, and mine did too.
I saw a little boy reflected there
who looked a lot like me.

I agreed with my father except
when Nana was there with us.
Then I agreed with my mother.
If my father was an orphan, Nana
would be a childless mother,
but she wasn't. She had my dad.

I lived in the middle of a family
riddle that lives in the middle of me.

GOING TO A CONFERENCE ON
WOMEN AND POVERTY

Holding coffee and a morning-glory
muffin, I stood in a line of women
waiting for half & half, skim or whole milk,
Splenda, raw, brown or white sugar.
A snow-sprinkled fuzzy red cap dripping
on salt and pepper hair grabbed my eye
from across the room. I looked away
from the woman under the cap gripping
a rusted cart overflowing
with dented soda cans, plastic bags,
ripped newspapers, and a thin
brown blanket peeking out from under
a dirty torn tarp. I put my hand
in my pocket, but it came back empty.

I rushed next door to the conference.
She must have sneaked in behind me,
stayed out of sight all day, shadowed me
to the car, crawled into the back seat,
slipped out and slipped into the breezeway.
She won't leave, but mostly stays out of sight.
Today she popped up on the way
to the supermarket. She yelled. I jumped.
We passed a man holding a ragged piece
of cardboard, words barely visible,
I'll work for food   help me   God bless.
I turned around, but it was too late.

HOME

Kinder, küche, kirche—
kindness, caring, sharing,
home, heart, hearth.

Home is a place, a roof overhead—
safe haven from the storm or in
harm's way? It's hard to say.

Home is enough grub, 3 squares a day—
does it matter if you have a say
in what you would eat, and where you'd be?

Home is family, generations,
traditions—but must progeny
and love be conditions?

Home is a room of one's own—
does it have to feel like home
and what if you're all alone?

"Home is . . . where, when you . . . go there,
they have to take you in."[1] By choice,
rejoice! Without choice, rejoice?

Home is roots, rootless, rest, restless,
ties that bind and ties that free—
trapped or freed, want or need?

Maybe home is more—home bliss, home bless.
Maybe home is less—homeless.
Homeless you may be yourself, you know.

Home is where the heart is.
Traveling companion you can't leave
behind, home is rooted in place—
and there's no place like home.

1. Excerpt from "The Death of the Hired Man," Robert Frost (1923)

SWIMMING

Move into the corpse position,
the yoga teacher said. Startled,
I pictured you the way you were
the last time that I saw you.
The music shifts to water sounds
as ocean waves wash over me
bringing you back, swimming.

Giant crab-like hands and wing-like arms
set the pace and lead the way.
Strong strokes cut deep slicing choppy waters,
churning the sea. Foot paddles
flap so fast your flutter kick leaves
a wake making a path for me, Daddy.
My little feet flutter, flounder,
flutter as you teach me to swim.

Back then you never swam too far,
always stayed near enough I knew
that I'd make it back to shore.

BREATHING

The teacher says, *Breathe. Relax your face,*
shoulders, arms, legs, all of you.
Breathing in the rhythm of the sounds
I move in, out, and beyond myself.
Stretch your arms. Make a big circle
as if you're hugging a tree.

The tree has a life of its own.
Out of nowhere you are there
in the marrow—your eyes sparkling black,
your face bony, your cheeks ruddy
but not from sun or air. You're wearing
that big black hoodie, the one you wore
to ward off chills you knew were not outside,
the one you wore to hide your puffed up gut,
the one you wore to shield us from the thing
that even you could not fix.
You're still beaming that impish grin.

The teacher's voice uproots you, Michael.
Sweet brother, I breathe both of us here.

GRACE PERIOD

Grace period—
I like the concept very much,
the notion that someone would trust
me, at least awhile, cut me
some slack, no need to watch my back.
I'm not late. No one's irate—I rate!
Not rushed, relax, sit back, smile.
Graceful period in the middle of
hectic pace, deadlines, demands. Due dates,
due dates, due dates. Do, do, don't
have to show up, give up, pay up, grow up,
not yet, not today, not this minute,
hour, second, or season. Something
for nothing—nothing for some things.
The curtain will wait, no interest
accumulates, the book's not due.
You can simply be—period free—
for a bit longer till you're stronger,
not pressed, till finished or dressed—rest—
not knowing when grace period again.
Grace. Period.

Happily, Happily

When I think of living
happily ever after
I think of a small white cottage
with bright blue trim
window boxes overflowing
pansies and petunias and peonies
flowers blooming everywhere

When I think of living
happily ever after
I think of living
with you

HER TERMS

Breasts, boobs, mounds, mountains, tits,
full, flat, round, pointing, sagging, dragging.

If only we had a different pair.
If only we were more or less endowed.
If only we could shape the svelte
or boyish body into something
else, anything but our own.
Fifties girls catapulted
into sixties women who morphed
to the millennium middle-aged
with few terms of endearment for our breasts.
Liberated and trapped in bodies freed
from bindings, corsets, and stays—
free to be with or without a bra,
but praying for more, or burdened
by big breasts treated like prey.

My grandmother, Nana, had
a large bosom, just one, her own.
It added to her stature.
Nana was fully endowed.

Promises

Eleanor
Eleanor Adele
Eleanor Adele Jean
Eleanor Adele Jean McMahon
Aunt Eleanor
Auntie El

You had no children of your own.
You had ten nieces and nephews
to love, and love us you did.

Whether from hundreds of miles
or around the corner from where
you lived, you were delighted
to see us every time we came,
and always wished we didn't have to leave.

You accepted me as I was,
not as you would have me be.
I never talked too much for you.
I never stayed too long.

You left a legacy of love.
I'll miss your quick ways and sure smile.
I have no children of my own.
I have twelve nieces and nephews—
and I have promises to keep.

Auntie El
Aunt Eleanor
Eleanor Adele Jean McMahon
Eleanor Adele Jean
Eleanor Adele
Eleanor

With These Hands

With these hands, I scoot and crawl
and pile up my blocks real tall.

With these hands, I hide my eyes
till Olivia says, *Surprise, surprise!*

With these hands, I touch your toys
until you make a big bad noise.

With these hands, I suck both thumbs
and soothe myself till someone comes.

With these hands, I drink my milk,
touch Blankie's edge that feels like silk.

With these hands, I play with Rose.
We touch our heads. We touch our toes.

With these hands, we play patty-cake.
With our crayons, giraffes we make.

With these hands, I dig in dirt
and rub them on my sister's shirt!

With these hands, I hug the best,
especially when I need a rest!

With these hands, I reach up high
and I wave, *Goodbye, goodbye!*

BABY BOY

Exhausted from protecting you from doors,
sockets, sharp edges, ledges, splinters—
from dancing you round and round
your music box, I fall breathless
into Gram's rocker, your Great Grammy.
You want to crawl, to explore the floor.

When you return, you pull yourself
up my mountainous leg scaling
from the foot to the ankle,
the calf, the knee, and the thigh.
You pause below the mountain's highest peak.
I cradle you in protective limbs,
your head resting on my chest.
Your breath breathes mine, mine yours.

How could it be that one day
you could be a soldier gone to war.

Emma's Song

Emma, who's four, makes maps for us,
her grand aunties, so we can find
the way from our house to hers,
and she from hers to ours.

All her maps have twists and turns,
lots of curves, a few dead ends.
Today, she drew her swimming pool
and made a *pretend one* for us.

Emma told us she's tired of snow,
wants winter to go. Then she sings,
Snow snow snow. Blow blow blow.
Snow snow snow. Go go go.

Ashton, her six-year-old brother, says,
That's not a song. I say, *It is a song.*
It's Emma's song, and we all sing.

Emma wants summer to come.
She wants to plant *lots of flowers,*
purple and pink, my favorite colors—
and orange, Ashton's favorite.

She wants to *plant watermelons,*
blackberries, and blueberries. She wants
to *watch the tomatoes grow tall.*

We want to watch Emma grow tall.
We want her to have it all!

Song for Myself

This is my life—
may I allow myself
to embrace all its

ups and downs
starts and stops
pieces and pains
loves and losses

down and up
stop and start
pain and peace
loss and love.

This is my life.

This is life.

HOW MANY ANGELS . . .

How many angels, you ask,
can dance on the head of a pin?

All of them. They take up no space.
They dance with grace. They never
step on toes so nobody knows
when they make mistakes, if they do.

No, none, not even one! They don't
have feet, can't move to a beat,
no booty to shake, no
body to move with the music.

All or none—why must it be one?
Refuse to choose! There's nothing to lose.
Like glimpsing sun, moon, a single star
moving across the sky, it depends where
they are when, and when you are where.

Forget questions. You don't need answers.
Invite them down. Give them some shoes
so they can dance on solid ground.
Listen to the music all around.

CLEARING THE LAND: COLLATERAL DAMAGE

digging down down   digging up blighted
potatoes crouched down crawling hunger
clawing   digging out   hauling boulders
clawing   digging out   hauling rocks
clawing   digging out hauling stones
hands down   hands up   hand over
digging deeper   scraping rock bottom
clearing the land   clearing their land
being cleared from their land   for pennies
for owners' crops   exports   profits
for someone else   somewhere else—
or crawling through   the poor house door
for scraps to eat   and a barn floor   for sleep
the cows' place for the best   who'd hobble
from there to city slums   and waste away—
the worst were carried up   up to the loft
saved for the sickest so   they'd die up high
saved so their bodies   could be
rolled   dumped   back to the land
that was theirs   back to the sordid
spoiled soil   spoils themselves
they laid claim   to the land
resting   finally   close to home

WATERS

Being middle-class, middle-age,
middle-western—and second born, second
daughter, second generation (or more)
white lace curtain American-Irish,
I listen to you, Tonya, who is
so young, say you are the "Oldest Oldest,"
and that you come from Alabama
and Nigeria and you're a scholar
and a runner to and from Lowell,
Massachusetts, and the world.

The first of my family, you say,
*not just mine, the whole family—
sisters, brother, cousins and the old ones,
not just my parents—aunts and uncles.
I am Oldest Oldest for the whole
family, for the whole generation.*

*It is a big responsibility.
I have always lived with it,
run with it, being oldest and first—
the first to grow up, to do new things,
to go away, and to go to college.*

*Soon I'll be the first, the very first,
to finish college. Soon I'll finish
for all of us, and for me.
It has taken a long time. Hard work.
It has not been easy. I can hardly
wait until I graduate in the spring.*

Just across the table, buds are bursting,
flowers blooming, and birds are singing.
I see them all around you, Tonya,
and feel the wind blowing fiercely
all the way from Nigeria.
Alabama breezes are whispering
to you, their Oldest Oldest.

When I do, Tonya says, raising up
her arms higher and higher,
*I'll kiss that plaque right on the stage
in front of everybody. I'll be
kissing that plaque for all of us
and for me, Oldest Oldest,
and first to finish college.*

Giselle, her friend, tells us that Tonya
will keep on keeping on.
She won't stop running. Giselle
asks Tonya what she'll do when she
gets her Master's. Tonya says,
*I'll be carrying buckets.
I'll be carrying two big buckets.*

Beyond the dark mums and white daisies
on the table, and a white gold-rimmed
china plate by your ruby-red napkin,
are plain old buckets weathered
by hottest seasons and coldest storms.

I see two big buckets hanging
from Tonya's strong young shoulders,
her Oldest Oldest shoulders.
The buckets are hanging heavy.
The buckets are swinging free.

I'll be carrying two big buckets
both full of tears—I'll be so happy
the buckets will be overflowing
with tears.
           The rush of the water
startles me, me so much older than you,
Tonya, and me never so old.
Being middle and being second,
I'm grateful to hear such sweet sweet sounds,
and to be near such holy waters.

GROWING HERE

Roads twist and turn opening on red,
purple, and white fuchsia hedges
growing wild above pungent pale pink
phlox, primrose-colored foxgloves,
and rainbow snaps. Whitewashed cottages
with blue and yellow doors behind
shouting orange, ruby, and whispering
peach rose bushes overlook
muddy brownish-black peat bogs
dug deep beside bricks stacked high.
All growing here, as I am.

Lover of small spaces, colors,
I expand in this land, stretch, rest,
grow full on old legacies and new grace.
Sheltered by stone walls, moss pillows,
I dream of quilts, comforters all shades
of green, more than my eyes had seen.
Washed by seas, dried with winds, rocked
by rowboats bobbing in Galway's Bay
and Dalkey's coves, home far away, and here.

FAMILY TREE

Since ancient African Goddess Isis
was the precursor of Mary, mother
of Jesus, does that make Anne,
mother of Mary, the sister
of Isis, and Isis God's
grandmother and godmother?

If so, does that make me, Anne's namesake,
the great-great-great-granddaughter
and goddaughter of all of them?

I hope so since then there's hope
for you and for me because
  we
      all
         must
            be
              related
                    somehow

and with those ancestors, you know
  we
      all
         come
            from
              a
                good
                  family.

This Morning

This morning, at the top of the stairs,
I spy half a heart—not even—
less than half a heart-shaped tricolored
eraser with a mini purple heart
in its center and faded red rubber
curved around its outer edge.
Layers of yellow and purple
nestle inside a dirty pink skin
worn down by daily duties—
wiping away errors, disappearing
small wrongs, inhaling lead, absorbing
toxins, sprouting an uneven
epidermis holding what's left
of the half heart that must have fallen
from my pocket yesterday.

I bend down, pick up the half heart,
and go down to today's mistakes.

TOMATOES

tomatoes are rotting
on the vine
hurry up
there's not much time
leave the dirt
shirk your work
let nature
take its course
as seasons pass
dusk is dawning
come inside
sit with me
let's be

KIERA'S HANDS

My niece Kiera molded her hands in clay
just weeks after her father, my brother,
died. The hands were delicate and strong.
They were so beautiful, I cried.
Each turned toward the other, fingers spread out
as if reaching for something large.

Kiera embedded the hands
in dark blue swirling clay.
Strange shapes held fingers, knuckles, nails.
Churning bits of white-edged indigo blue
waves crested over an angry sea.

Deep black crevices slashed the ocean.
Layered blobs of twisted clay
morphed into a small blue rose
laid to rest on the fourth finger
of my niece Kiera's right hand.

Stepping back, the blue, though dark,
became wild lace edged in light.
I put Kiera's hands near the front door.
I wanted my dad to see what
she'd made as soon as he arrived.
I wanted to show him Kiera's hands,
offer him something hopeful–something,
if not happy, at least not sad.

My father, Kiera's grandfather, stumbled
as he crossed the threshold whacking
the hands with one of his—shattering
and scattering pieces and smithereens.
Kiera said, *It's okay. Throw them away.*
I said, *No, don't let them go!*
I picked up each piece, sliver, and shard.
I wanted to fix them, make things better.
I carried them home in a box.
After months, my partner said,
Throw them out, toss them, let them go.
No!, I said. Donna took them
to the attic where they stayed for years.

One day Donna took out all the pieces.
She remade the right hand aged by cracks
and reshaped the blue. The left hand
couldn't be saved, but bits of it remain.
Beyond the dining room table
up on a wall where it won't fall,
I see Kiera's right hand nestled
in midnight blue that sparkles in the sun.

Twenty-five years have come and gone.
Kiera's sons are six and four.
Their grandfather, Michael, is alive
in our hearts and in his grandsons' smiles.
We come from the same mold—my niece,
partner, me, you. We all have cracks.
Enough beauty. Enough blue.

ACKNOWLEDGMENTS

I am grateful to the editors of the following publications where a number of poems first appeared, sometimes as an earlier version.

"How Good It Was" was published in *Abafazi*. "On Turning 50" was published in the *Newburyport Art Association 50th Anniversary Cookbook*. "High Hopes Circa 1960" (titled "Teen Angels: High Hopes Circa 1960"), "For Patricia, Whose Hair I Straightened in 1962," and "Talking Back" were published in the *Powow River Poets Anthology II*. "At 80," "Change" (titled "Leona"), "Her Terms," and "Recycling" were published in *The Offering*. "Grace Period" was published in *The Undertoad*.

Had it not been for Jeri Kroll, this book would not have been written. She encouraged me to compile my poems and was with me every step of the way as publisher, editor, and much more. I am grateful for Jeri's wisdom, generosity, and amazing humor! I greatly appreciate Susan Kapuscinski Gaylord for her ongoing aesthetic and technical expertise, wise critiques, and encouragement. Susan also designed this beautiful book and its artful cover.

I thank Beth Munro for her technical, editorial, and grammatical assistance—and her good humor. Many thanks to Kathy Desilets and Irene Egan for their help and support on this and many other projects. I am fortunate to have wonderful friends and to belong to great "families" including the Mulvey and O'Neill clans, the Powow River Poets, Amherst Writers & Artists, InterPlay, UMass Lowell, and the greater Lowell community. Thank you all for sharing your stories and encouraging me to share mine.

My greatest gratitude and love go to Donna O'Neill—life partner, spouse, and resident critic in the best sense of the word. Thank you for your patience and kindness during yet another big project in the middle of moving and the pandemic. You are the best!

ABOUT THE AUTHOR

Anne Mulvey began writing poetry in response to her brother Michael's death in 1994. Her poems have been published in *Abafazi*, *The Bridge Review*, *The Community Psychologist*, *The Offering*, *The Powow River Poets Anthology II*, and grassroots publications. Anne, Professor Emerita of Psychology at the University of Massachusetts Lowell, has incorporated poetry and creative writing into academic courses and community-based projects. She is certified as an Amherst Writers & Artists leader and an InterPlay leader. A long-time member of the Powow River Poets in Newburyport, Massachusetts, Anne lives in Groveland with her spouse, Donna O'Neill, and their rescue dog, Bitsie.

Made in the USA
Middletown, DE
25 February 2021